AMAZING ARCHITECTURE
AMAZING
SKYSCRAPERS

by Anita Nahta Amin

pogo

Ideas for Parents and Teachers

Pogo Books let children practice reading informational text while introducing them to nonfiction features such as headings, labels, sidebars, maps, and diagrams, as well as a table of contents, glossary, and index.

Carefully leveled text with a strong photo match offers early fluent readers the support they need to succeed.

Before Reading

- "Walk" through the book and point out the various nonfiction features. Ask the student what purpose each feature serves.
- Look at the glossary together. Read and discuss the words.

Read the Book

- Have the child read the book independently.
- Invite him or her to list questions that arise from reading.

After Reading

- Discuss the child's questions. Talk about how he or she might find answers to those questions.
- Prompt the child to think more. Ask: Have you seen a skyscraper? What features did it have to fight the force of wind?

Pogo Books are published by Jump!
5357 Penn Avenue South
Minneapolis, MN 55419
www.jumplibrary.com

Copyright © 2023 Jump!
International copyright reserved in all countries. No part of this book may be reproduced in any form without written permission from the publisher.

Library of Congress Cataloging-in-Publication Data

Names: Amin, Anita Nahta, author.
Title: Amazing skyscrapers / by Anita Nahta Amin.
Description: Minneapolis, MN: Jump!, Inc. [2023]
Series: Amazing architecture
Includes index. | Audience: Ages 7-10.
Identifiers: LCCN 2022004473 (print)
LCCN 2022004474 (ebook)
ISBN 9781636907444 (hardcover)
ISBN 9781636907451 (paperback)
ISBN 9781636907468 (ebook)
Subjects: LCSH: Skyscrapers—Juvenile literature.
Skyscrapers—Design and construction—Juvenile literature.
Classification: LCC TH1615 .A45 2023 (print)
LCC TH1615 (ebook) | DDC 720/.483—dc23/eng/20220203
LC record available at https://lccn.loc.gov/2022004473
LC ebook record available at https://lccn.loc.gov/2022004474

Editor: Eliza Leahy
Designer: Molly Ballanger

Photo Credits: Laborant/Shutterstock, cover; Mlenny/iStock, 1; Jeffrey Liao/Shutterstock, 3; Ingus Kruklitis/Shutterstock, 4; archiZG/iStock, 5 (blueprint); Kucher Serhii/Shutterstock, 5 (background); KangeStudio/iStock, 6-7; Kertu/Shutterstock, 8; Rajesh Vijayakumar/Shutterstock, 9; Kubrak78/iStock, 10-11; Horst Petzold/Dreamstime, 12-13; Eugene Lu/Shutterstock, 14; ansonmiao/iStock, 15; S-F/Shutterstock, 16-17; Nisian Hughes/Getty, 18-19; Aniczkania/Shutterstock, 20-21; dibrova/Shutterstock, 23.

Printed in the United States of America at Corporate Graphics in North Mankato, Minnesota.

Title Page Image: Bahrain World Trade Center, Bahrain

TABLE OF CONTENTS

Taipei 101,
Taiwan

CHAPTER 1

SCRAPE THE SKY

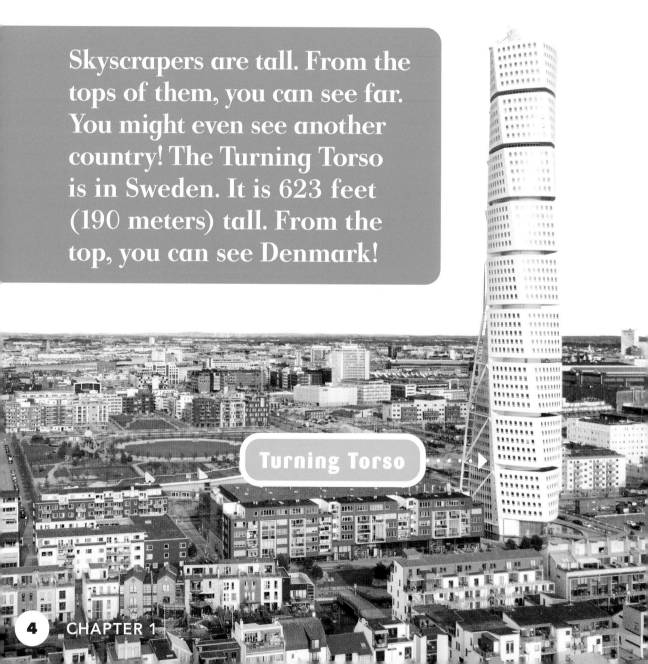

Skyscrapers are tall. From the tops of them, you can see far. You might even see another country! The Turning Torso is in Sweden. It is 623 feet (190 meters) tall. From the top, you can see Denmark!

Turning Torso

blueprint

Architects design skyscrapers. They make **blueprints**. These show how the buildings will look.

Engineers make **models**. They test the models in **wind tunnels**. This shows if a building will stand in wind. Then, construction workers build the skyscrapers.

model

....

CHAPTER 2

WIND AND LOAD

Skyscrapers have to stand up to the **force** of wind. To do this, they are built to sway slightly. Otherwise, they would break.

blow-through floor

Some buildings have blow-through floors. These are open to the air. Wind blows through. This lessens the force of wind on the building.

Willis Tower

Uneven shapes or **surfaces** break up wind flow. Willis Tower is in Chicago, Illinois. It is made of tubes. They are different heights. Wind hits different parts of the tower at different times.

TAKE A LOOK!

How do Willis Tower's tubes spread out wind force?
Take a look!

---→ = **WIND**

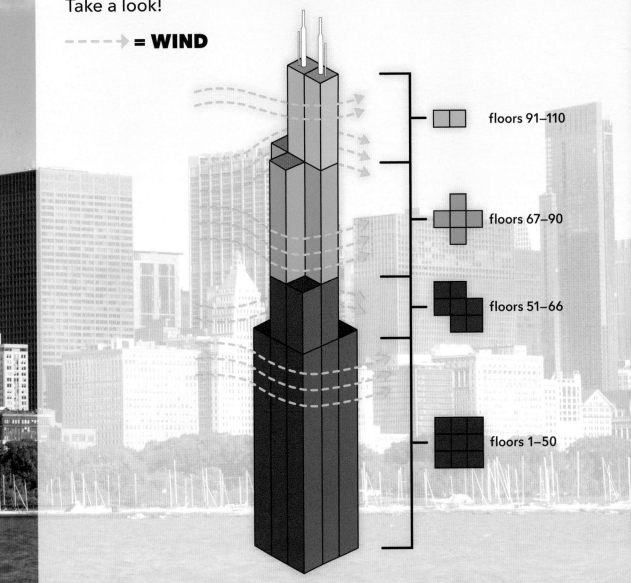

floors 91–110

floors 67–90

floors 51–66

floors 1–50

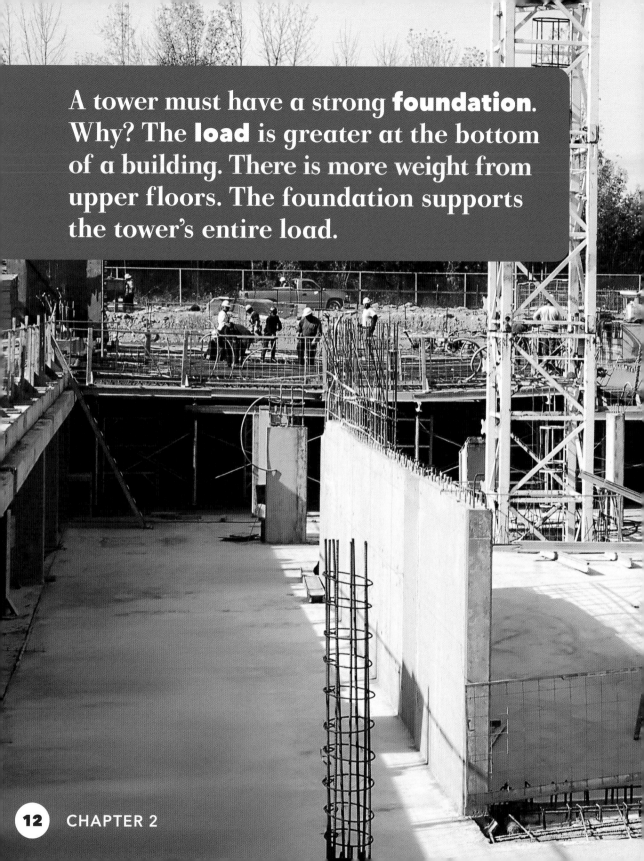

A tower must have a strong **foundation**. Why? The **load** is greater at the bottom of a building. There is more weight from upper floors. The foundation supports the tower's entire load.

TAKE A LOOK!

. . . .

Piles can be part of a foundation. They help support the load of a building. Take a look!

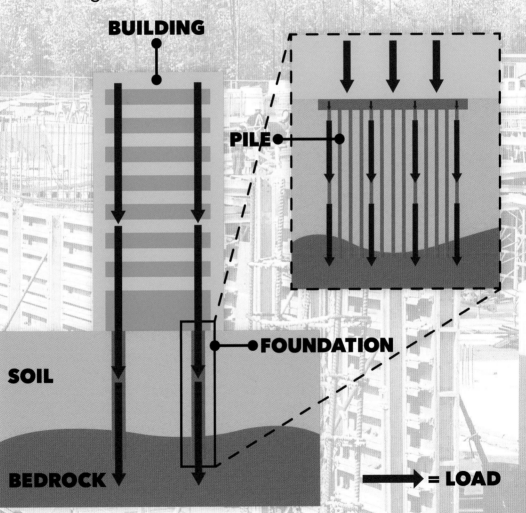

BUILDING

PILE

FOUNDATION

SOIL

BEDROCK

→ = LOAD

CHAPTER 3

· ·

FAMOUS SKYSCRAPERS

Shanghai Tower is in China.
It rises 2,073 feet (632 m).
It has a deep, thick foundation.
This helps it stand in soft soil.

Shanghai
Tower · · · · · ▶

The tower has to stand up to **typhoons**. These storms bring high winds. The tower has round edges. They lessen the force of wind on the building.

spire ·····▸

Burj
Khalifa ·····▸

The Burj Khalifa is in Dubai, United Arab Emirates. It is the tallest building in the world! It is 2,717 feet (828 m) tall. Its **spire** is more than 700 feet (213 m) tall. It sends lightning down to the ground. This keeps the building safe if it is hit.

The Burj Khalifa is built on sand. Its bottom is wide for better support. Underground, 192 piles support the building.

DID YOU KNOW?

It took about six years to build the Burj Khalifa. More than 12,000 people worked on it.

Steinway Tower is in New York City. It is also known as 111 West 57th Street. It is a pencil tower. This means it is tall and thin. It is 1,428 feet (435 m) tall. But it is only 60 feet (18 m) wide.

Panels and **lattices** make the surface uneven. This lessens the force of wind on the tower.

DID YOU KNOW?

A damper is a heavy weight attached to a building. It **absorbs** wind force. Steinway Tower has one. It is heavier than 100 elephants!

Steinway
Tower

Gherkin

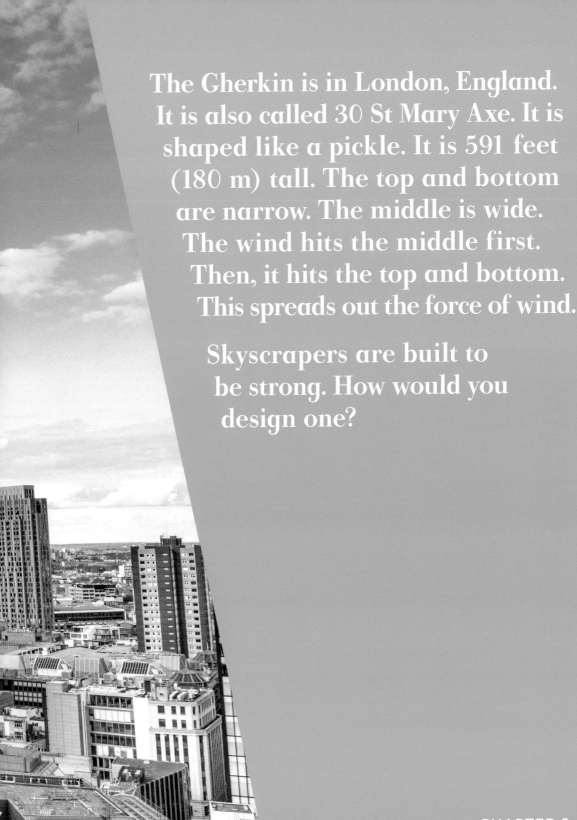

The Gherkin is in London, England. It is also called 30 St Mary Axe. It is shaped like a pickle. It is 591 feet (180 m) tall. The top and bottom are narrow. The middle is wide. The wind hits the middle first. Then, it hits the top and bottom. This spreads out the force of wind.

Skyscrapers are built to be strong. How would you design one?

ACTIVITIES & TOOLS

BUILD A SKYSCRAPER

See how the force of wind affects skyscrapers in this fun activity!

What You Need:

- building blocks or cardboard boxes
- ruler
- small fan
- timer
- paper
- pen or pencil

1. Using building blocks or cardboard boxes, build a tower without any gaps.

2. Using a ruler, measure a spot 1 foot (0.3 meters) from your tower. Set a fan there.

3. Start a timer and turn on the fan. Record how long it takes for the tower to blow over.

4. Build another tower. This time, leave gaps between some of the blocks.

5. Repeat Step 3. Does the tower blow down? If so, how long does it take? Why do you think this is?

6. Change the shape of the tower or use other materials to build another tower. Is the tower stronger or weaker? Why do you think this is?

GLOSSARY

absorbs: Takes in.

architects: People who design the look of structures.

blueprints: Models or detailed sketches of how structures will look.

engineers: People who are specially trained to design and build machines or large structures.

force: An action that produces, stops, or changes the shape or movement of an object.

foundation: A solid base on which a structure is built.

lattices: Structures with crisscrossed patterns.

load: The amount carried at one time.

models: Things architects or engineers build or design as examples of larger structures.

panels: Flat pieces of wood or other materials made to form part of a surface such as a wall.

piles: Heavy wood or steel beams that are driven into the ground to help support a structure.

spire: A structure that comes to a point at the top.

surfaces: The outermost layers of things.

typhoons: Violent tropical storms with high winds and rain that occur in the western Pacific Ocean.

wind tunnels: Machines that produce heavy winds and are used to test a building's strength.

INDEX

TO LEARN MORE

Finding more information is as easy as 1, 2, 3.

1 Go to www.factsurfer.com

2 Enter "amazingskyscrapers" into the search box.

3 Choose your book to see a list of websites.

FACT SURFER